Bosco and Kitty's PIANO MAGIC

By Robert Pace

Illustrations by Roberta Wilson

LR Lee Roberts Music Publications, Inc.
Chatham, New York

Bosco Barker, a happy young puppy, and Kitty Purrmew, a playful calico kitten, were very good friends who lived in a big, old house with a beautiful piano in it.

They both loved the high and low sounds of their piano, which they could make by pressing down the "Twins and Triplets" – the groups of two and three black keys.

But Kitty and Bosco were quite different. Outside in the yard, Kitty loved to climb up, up, up, in her favorite tall tree, then scamper back down to see what Bosco was doing.

Bosco's fun was to make a big leap and splash into the fish pond – going down, down, down, and quickly back up to find Kitty. He liked to see her face as he jumped out, spraying water everywhere.

Kitty had many friends in her tree – bluebirds, squirrels, and bear cubs – that she wanted to share with Bosco. And he had some water friends – the fish, turtles, and ducks – that he wanted to share with Kitty. These were their "Twins and Triplets friends." But how could they share their friends, since Bosco couldn't climb a tree, and Kitty didn't know how to swim?

Suddenly, a brilliant idea came to both of them. "Let's just pretend that we are going high in the tree, or low in the water to find these friends, and like magic, the piano Twins and Triplets can become the Twins and Triplets of the tree and the pond. That's our PIANO MAGIC!"

So Kitty started in the middle of the piano and went up to find the high Twins. Carefully, she went up the keyboard, one paw at a time, touching only the Twins, as if she were climbing her favorite tree. When she got to the top, she waited a moment, then pressed the very top Twins again. Gradually, paw over paw, she touched each set of Twins as she came back to the middle of the piano.

"Now, Bosco – it's your turn." So he moved to the middle of the piano, but as he pressed the first set of Twins, he said, "Wow – my paw is awfully big for these little Twins."

Kitty said, "Don't be silly, you can do almost anything if you really try!" So he really tried, and sure enough, he found all of the Twins as he went higher to the top, and back again to the middle of the keyboard.

"That was great!" said Bosco. "Now, let me show you the Triplets going down, down, down." He took his big paw and pressed the Triplets near the middle of the keyboard, then the next set lower, and still lower to the bottom. As he started upward, he imagined that he was *really* in the pond with his Triplet friends.

8

When Bosco returned to the middle, he woofed, "Now, Kitty, it is your turn to find all of the lower Triplets." Kitty carefully put her paw on the Triplets in the middle of the piano, then meowed, "Bosco, I don't think my paw is big enough to cover the Triplets."

Smiling, he said, "Just remember – you can do almost anything if you really try!" That did it – those were her own words! So without another "meow," she found every set of Triplets from the middle of the keyboard to the bottom and back to the middle again. "So there, Bosco, of course I can do it!"

Finding the low Triplets was so much fun that Kitty decided she would find all of the Triplets from the middle to the very top of the keyboard. She found the first set of Triplets, then slowly moved over the Twins to put her paw just above on the next Triplets. As she pressed on them, they made a nice sound that was different from the first Triplets – it was higher.

Kitty suddenly got a funny look on her face as she pressed the first Triplets again, then the higher Triplets. "This is most interesting," she thought, and she decided to try them again. But this time, after she pressed the lower Triplets, she made a long "m–e–o–w, then quickly pressed the higher Triplets.

"Bosco – guess what? I have just discovered that my meow is somewhere between these two sets of Triplets."

"Great!" said Bosco, "now that you have found your meow, would you please find the rest of the Triplets, so I can have my turn?"

When Kitty got back to the middle, she said, "Okay, Bosco. It's your turn. But don't be so grumpy!"

"I'm not grumpy," said Bosco. "It's just that you have found where your meow is, so now I'd like to find my woof." Then, up to the top of the keyboard he went, finding all of the Triplets, and back again to the middle. But he didn't hear any Triplets that seemed near his woof.

"Kitty, maybe I should go lower to find where my woof is. I'll start here in the middle and listen to all of the lower Twins." He carefully moved over the Triplets and pressed the Twins just below them. He liked their sound, but he wanted to hear all of the lower Twins, so he moved down to the next set. He went still lower until he reached the lowest Twins, then up again. He listened carefully to each, but none seemed close to his woof, until he got back to the very first one. When he heard it, he got so excited that he went "woof, woof, woof!" Kitty called out, "That's it, Bosco – you've found your woof. *Your* voice is lower than mine."

Kitty liked to try new things, so she said, "Let's have more magic and play *Hide and Seek* with the Twins and Triplets."

"How can we do that?" asked Bosco. Kitty thought a moment, then said, "First, let's pretend that we are hiding the Twins. Close your eyes, then reach out and feel the black keys until you have two that you think are Twins. Next, open your eyes to see if you were correct. Then, close your eyes and find another set of Twins higher or lower."

But, my big paw – " complained Bosco. Kitty quickly reminded him, "Of course you can do it if you really try." She was right!

After a few tries, Bosco became really good at finding the higher Twins. "This is great fun! Now it's your turn, Kitty. How about finding some of the lower Twins?" he said, with a smile and a short "woof."

Kitty couldn't wait – she found a set of Twins below the middle of the keyboard, then another set a little lower and one more set really low.

"Now, I am going to find them again as I come back up," she said.

"Kitty, you are really good! Now begin in the middle and play *Hide and Seek* with all of the Triplets to the top."

As usual she said, "Bosco, my small paws..." He would have no part of that, but before he could remind Kitty, she said, "I know, I know – I can do almost anything if I really try. So I will do it!"

She then hid and found all of the Triplets from the middle to the top, and back again without a single mistake.

"What fun! We should play this every day."

And, so they did.

One fine morning after breakfast, Kitty said, "Bosco, let's do some more magic and pretend that you are diving 'way down in the water to play *Hide and Seek* with your Triplet friends. But really you will do this with the lower keyboard Triplets.

He thought that was a great idea. So he pretended that he jumped into the water. He found the first set, then another set, and further down, even one more set of Triplets. Like a fish, he started up again, and found all of the keyboard Triplets to the middle.

"Hey, Kitty, I just had an idea for a game," said Bosco. "You start at the top of the keyboard and I will start at the bottom to find all of the Triplets. When we finish, you will be at the bottom and I will be at the top."

"Okay," said Kitty, "and be sure you don't peek!"

Quick as a wink, they started toward each other to find the Triplets from one end of the piano to the other. When they reached opposite ends, they both called out, "This is fun! Let's try it with Triplets one day and Twins the next."

Several days later, Kitty had a new idea. "Bosco, you start at the bottom and cover the lowest Twins with your left paw and the next set of Triplets with your right paw. At the same time, I will cover the highest Twins with my right paw and the Triplets just below with my left paw. Then we'll close our eyes and find both Twins and Triplets all the way to the middle.

They closed their eyes and gently pressed the Twins, then the Triplets, to get the sound and feel of each. They played them several times, then moved to the next Twins and Triplets, and pressed them to get their sounds. As they reached the middle of the keyboard, Kitty opened her eyes and said, "Bosco, look! There is only one set of Twins left."

One morning as Kitty started down the stairs, Bosco thought, "I'll begin at the top and play a Triplet, then a Twin as she steps down the stairs." When Kitty arrived at the bottom of the stairs, Bosco also arrived at the bottom of the keyboard. "There must be the same number of Triplets and Twins as there are stair steps," said Bosco. "To find out," said Kitty "start on the bottom Twins and go slowly to the top and back down as I step up and down the stairs."

As they returned to the bottom, Kitty remarked, "If I run up and down, you will need to play them faster."

"That's right," said Bosco. "We can make our Triplets and Twins go slow or fast as they move higher or lower. First, go up and down slowly, then try it a little faster."

"Let's play a new game of *Hide and Seek*," suggested Kitty. "Close your eyes as I play either the Twins twice, or the Triplets three times. Then you find and play them *just as loud or soft* as I did." They tried it and Bosco got each one right on the first try.

"Now, play Twins that are *high and* also *slow*," said Kitty. "I will play them twice very slowly to give you their sound, then you find and play them exactly as I did – *no faster or slower* and *no louder or softer*."

Again, Bosco got each right and couldn't wait for Kitty's turn.

Bosco sounded low Triplets three times quickly, as Kitty listened. Then she covered those same Triplets and played them exactly as he had done. "That was *purrfect*, Kitty! Now we can try them every way from *very, very slow* to *very, very fast* as we go high or low and make them loud or soft.

One warm summer afternoon, as Bosco snoozed under the piano and Kitty cat-napped on top, there was a huge *c r a s h – b o o m* of thunder that shook everything in the house.

Kitty said, "That's the loudest noise I have ever heard." "Rrrr-wow!" said Bosco, "It was *very low, very loud* and *very slow*. It sounded like this..." he said, playing the lowest Triplets of the piano three times with both paws, to make it as loud as possible."

"I'd like to try the thunder, also." said Kitty, as she found the same Triplets, then made a very low, loud, and slow *b o o m*! Bosco clapped his paws and said, "Kitty – you make super thunder!"

Kitty looked outside and said, "Bosco, raindrops are beginning to fall. I will make the higher Twins sound like little drops of water splashing softly here and there. As the rain falls faster and becomes louder, I will move to the middle of the keyboard." "Terrific!" said Bosco, "I will make thunder when you want it. But what happens when the rain and thunder quit?"

Kitty replied quickly, "Don't worry about that, Bosco. Since we can go *High and Low, Loud* and *Soft, and Fast and Slow* with our Twins and Triplets, we can create more new musical stories just like magic. Who knows, we may even find a rainbow."

And so, each day they played a new game.

One fine day, soon after all of the thunder and rain, Bosco and Kitty were enjoying some of their piano magic on the Twins and Triplets when Kitty asked, "Would you like to make up some stories and play songs that use both the black and white keys of the piano?" Bosco replied, "Sure, that will be easy now that we can find our way all over the keyboard with the Twins and Triplets. But there is one condition -- will we still be partners, so we can help each other if we have problems?" "Of course," Kitty purred happily, "it's much more fun that way." Then they both began thinking of all the new Piano Magic they could create.